Hazy Red and Diesel Grey

Travis Blair

Old Seventy Creek Press
Albany, Kentucky

Acknowledgments

Many thanks to the journals and publications in which these poems or versions of these poems first appeared:

Bohemia Literary Journal: "After Hours"
Cenizo: "Cats and Colors"
ckinggalleries: "Blues Song"
First Literary Review-East: "Winged Sonata"
Gutter Eloquence Magazine: "My Father's Eyes," "Twenty-Eights"
Illya's Honey: "Crossing the Border," "Kissing Booth," "It Never Rains in Cairo," "Along Randol Mill Road"
Poetry at Round Top: "Texas Vampires"
Red Fez Magazine: "Best Bitch," "Busting Out of Balmorhea," "Del Rio, Two AM"
Red River Review: "Hospital Vamp," "One Year After Her Father Died," "Black & White Photo of Mom, 1942," "Everything's OK on the LBJ," "Departures," "Mogen David and Fifty Shades," "Breakfast on the Beach," "Finn's Grill & Icehouse"
Rusty Truck: "Crossing the Desert"
San Pedro River Review: "I Drove the Ramones to Rock'n'Roll High School"
Texas Poetry Calendar: "Blue Norther," "Cooking With Secrets"
Windmills (Australia): "A Graffiti of Bats"
Yellow Mama: "Growing Up in West Dallas"

Thanks to Ann Howells, Jeffrey Alfier and Michelle Hartman for the time and suggestions they gave in editing and helping revise these poems. Thanks to Larry D. Thomas for his encouragement and suggestions.

Special thanks to my friend and publisher Rudy Thomas at Old Seventy Creek Press who always gives me the freedom to write and create poems and manuscripts, then hands me a top-notch finished product from his fabulous publishing company.

Other books by Travis Blair
from Old Seventy Creek Press
Train to Chihuahua
Little Sandwiches

Cover Design/Photograph by John Lee Hunter

2014, Old Seventy Creek First Edition
Printed in the United States of America

ISBN -13: 978-0692304044
ISBN -10: 0692304045

*Old Seventy Creek Press is small,
but it is a press in search of words that have
been cut from the hide of a passing moment.*

Old Seventy Creek Press
Rudy Thomas, Editor & Publisher
P.O. Box 204
Albany, Kentucky 42602

for Mom

who taught me
women are tougher than men

Mom and her younger brother, 1942, Dallas

Black & White Photo of Mom, 1942

Barely 18, arm slacked
around your younger brother's neck
one day before he set sail for the Pacific,
you look so carefree. No thought
of Japanese bombs on Pearl Harbor.
Spending your days jerking sodas
behind a Skillern's lunch counter,
you haven't thought of me yet,
haven't married my father.
You are brash, sexy,
a year away from wedding vows.

Soon you'll surrender your breasts
to a red-haired Fort Worth flyboy
before sending him off in his B-24
to wreak havoc, Burma to Australia.
Two years later you'll offer me
my first taste of soft warm nipple,
forever impacting
what I love about women.
Who knew what power
your bosom wielded
when you leaned into this picture,
young and cocky, posing
for bigger than Life photographs
like a fledgling movie star.

Table of Contents

Hazy Red and Diesel Grey

Growing Up in West Dallas

Summer afternoons when I was thirteen
I'd sit on a patch of grass beneath
an open window outside my Daddy's
West Dallas honky tonk.

Too young to go inside and play the jukebox
or join daddy eating pickled eggs at the bar
I'd shoot marbles with my brother
or fling those little barbed grass spears
at alley cats running
into the old city cemetery next door

—not your average graveyard
with the Barrows brothers buried there
riddled full of bullet holes
from their Bonnie and Clyde days.

Some afternoons we'd sit
in daddy's pink Lincoln Continental
watch the hookers and whores strut
up and down Fort Worth Avenue

see them climb into cars and park
near the rear of the cemetery
where they'd go down on Johns
or straddle them for fifty dollars.

Some evenings when the sun set
all hazy red and diesel grey
the girls strutted over and leaned
into daddy's Lincoln land yacht
chewing gum and blowing bubbles
smelling like cum
making my brother and me
feel all hot and grown up

until daddy hollered through the window
for them to come inside and hit the stage
(I guess that's where my affection
for strippers and whores began)

Last Sunday I drove by
daddy's old honkey tonk—
now a used car lot
painted rust brown and selling Chevys—

stopped to walk among the graves.
Gone are Buck and Clyde's headstones
(stolen by some thrill seekers)
Gone are the hookers and strippers.
Gone is daddy
standing inside the open window
cracking boiled egg shells.

But I can still remember
the music on the jukebox
the smell of cum on breath
and the alley cats
running through the graveyard.

Cooking With Secrets

Grandma lived in her kitchen,
cooked on an old Glenwood stove—
fried chicken, cobblers, her Dr Pepper
Cocoa-Butter Sheet Cakes. All the kids
in the neighborhood feasted on her treats

at a cherrywood table set against the wall,
a relic from the Menger Hotel. Her Persian cat
Archie basked in the kitchen window, leered
at birds daring a song in her cottonwoods
while she told familiar stories, fingerprints

from her youth. Between the table and stove
hung an autographed photo— Teddy Roosevelt,
back in the days when he led the Rough Riders
down in San Antonio. Grandma flashed a tiny
grin when asked about the picture, hummed

the grace of a quiet sigh, and said nothing.
She turned back to the coal born flames, winked
at Archie, kept her secrets to herself. She moved
with a hint of flirty mirth, her footsteps
echoing through the kitchen.

Kissing Booth

You'd never see it today
but in 1960 a kissing booth
at Oak Cliff Carnival
made money hand over fist
for Red Cross' Emergency
Tornado Relief Fund.

Nineteen-year-old Molly Stone,
Miss Fourth of July Fire Cracker,
boldly stood selling kisses—
one dollar for up to six seconds.
A lengthier kiss cost you five.

I was just a kid and she
way out of my class, but I had
twenty dollars to spend.
I screwed up my courage, got in line.
A couple of dollar kisses
nearly made me faint. She laughed
when I returned for a third
and slipped her a five.

Last time in line I handed her
a ten, whispered *Can you make me
remember this one the rest of my life?*
She grinned and hung one on me
that's stuck in my memory to this day—
tongue and soft lips and serious grind,
a train crash, locomotive hurled
into trees, my woods on fire!

I was so dizzy when Molly let go,
my buddies had to grab me by the arms
and help me stagger back to the car.

For Whites Only

In 1968 I was a young preacher
at a country church in Alvarado,
a tiny Texas town. My congregation
never numbered a hundred
but I gave 'em both barrels every Sunday
as though I were Billy Graham
preaching to thousands.

Four years
into LBJ's Civil Rights Act,
the water fountain in the square
still declared *For Whites Only*
and not a dark-skinned child
dared take a drink to quench his thirst
on a hot summer day.

The washateria on the road into town
had a back door to a back room
with two old washers and a single drier
for coloreds (not clothes, but people)
Whites Only were allowed in front.

The week Martin Luther King died,
murdered at a Memphis motel,
I sat studying my sermon
in the back of the sanctuary
and heard the men in Sunday School
say *That nigger*
got what he deserved.

I walked to the pulpit
that sad morning
and told them *That nigger*
was a man just like me.
A Christian, a preacher,

a father, and I'm
not going to dignify
this gathering with my presence.

I strode down the center aisle
out the door and drove away.
That night they apologized.
A month later they fired me.

Just as well.
Even in 1968 I didn't fit
into their *Whites Only* world.

My Father's Eyes

Of all places
in a land as big as Texas
I encountered him on the bridge
crossing over from Eagle Pass
into Piedras Negras.

He was walking out of Mexico
his arm around a girl
half his age.
They smelled of whiskey
and old fish.

He grinned when he saw me
but his eyes didn't smile.
What are you doing here?
he asked.

I've come to film the bull fights,
I answered with an awkward
shuffle of feet.

He introduced me
to Ann Marie who told me
I possessed my father's eyes.
I never mentioned her
to mom, of course,
nor anyone else.

Now when I get caught
doing things I shouldn't,
I grin and wonder if my eyes
are as transparent
as my father's.

After Hours

When I was young
after hours meant Mother Blues,
that infamous house on Lemmon Avenue.
You never knew who might drop in.
I remember seeing David Bowie, Alice Cooper,
young Robert Plant – shirt unbuttoned,
showing off his bare Led Zeppelin chest.

Once I watched Janis Joplin toke a fat one
with T-Bone Walker before snatching the stage
and bringing down the house with *Ball and Chain*.
After Janis, I left because that was as good
as it was gonna get, and who can resist
Waffle House at 4AM when you're stoned
and pissing the blues.

I Drove the Ramones to
Rock'n'Roll High School

They strolled off the plane at Love Field, punk
as drainpipe trousers. I introduced myself to Joey—
the one wearing rose-colored shades.
I'm here to check you into the Melrose,
drive you to the midnight premiere, and ask you
please don't trash your hotel suite.
I was sent to fetch them because I sported
the longest hair. On our way to my Lincoln
Convertible Joey asked, *You got any weed?*
I handed him an alligator-covered cigarette case
filled with Tommy Chong sized joints.
Try not to smoke 'em all in one place and, please,
don't trash your hotel suite.

Inside the Esquire Theatre, everyone floated
higher than a helium-filled full moon.
When end credits rolled, the Ramones bowed
to the crowd, mostly screaming teenage girls
who rushed the stage. I shoved the boys out
the back door and we sped away to Mother Blues.
Thin Lizzy rocked that legendary stage
and the Ramones joined them for a stoned version
of *I Wanna Be Sedated*. Afterwards, we drove
downtown to see where Kennedy was assassinated.
On our way, Joey found half a dozen light sabers
left over from our *Star Wars* promotion.
And below the infamous sixth floor window,
the Ramones drew their sabers
and battled the Evil Empire.

When the band flew out Sunday morning,
I heard the only trashing done to their hotel suite
was discarded light sabers and left over bodies
of a half-dozen storm troopers.

Blue Norther

Winter of '79 I fainted.
I remember walking
into an Amarillo 7-Eleven
out of a wind chill of five degrees
and snow blowing sideways
through barbed wire fences.

The heat inside the store
rushed my head like a cattle train.
I felt it coming and tried to sit
on a case of Texaco motor oil
but tumble-weeded head first
onto the concrete floor.

I woke up sprawled
as flat on my back as a hippie
high on Colombian redbud.
Strangers leaned over me,
wind-beaten West Texas faces
scrunched in concern. *You think
we should call an ambulance?*

No! I shook my head
as a cowboy pulled me to my feet.
It's just the flu, I lied
and hurried out the door.
That was thirty years ago
and I've remained
too embarrassed to visit
Amarillo again.

Cataclysms

2AM

Good to see you again, Darlin'
drawls the waitress with a twangy voice
and tattooed thighs. Her cleavage spills
like coffee from an over-filled pot. I don't
recognize her and I'm sure it's my first time
in this truckers' café.

She moves to the window, leans over the sill,
short skirt riding up to reveal black panties.
I can't help staring at her silk-covered vee.

Would you look at that moon! Her mock gasp
makes me snicker. She glances over a shoulder,
catches my stare, gives a knowing wink with
laugh-wrinkled Alice Cooper eyes. She says
You always had a naughty mind, smoothes
her skirt, devours me with a rapacious gaze.

Flicking crumbs with a lacquered nail,
she asks, *Do you remember that necklace
I wore? You know, cross on a silver chain?
I gave it to my ex. Well, he drowned.*

I'm sorry, I offer, and after a pause,
When did it happen?

Last year, she whispers, eyes tearing.
*He died in that Indian Ocean tsunami.
Do you think the moon on the tides
caused all that?*

No. It was a natural cataclysm, I respond,
and rest my hand on her knee.

23

She looks across the table, whispers
with quivering lips, *Do you know how much
you remind me of him?* Her eyes ask me
to spend the night.

4AM

I lie in bed smoking a cigarette, looking
out the window. An egg yolk moon wanders
across a West Texas sky. She lies beside me,
bathed in moonlight, covered with sweat.
What's a cataclysm?

*A violent upheaval—like an earthquake,
a flood, a tsunami. It causes devastation.*

She's silent for a moment, fingers stroking
my chest. *I have suffered cataclysms*, she utters.
I pull her into a tight embrace. She slides on top,
her mouth covering mine with want
as I fill her with forget.

7AM

I stand shirtless, zipping my jeans. The moon
rides low as Sunday morning stirs in sleep.
Behind me, she sprawls in bed, and I wonder
if her dreams are peaceful.

I think of the tsunami and all the dead,
the grief. People asking what's to blame?
I light a cigarette, exhale it slowly,
watch the smoke swirl in chaotic circles.

It Never Rains in Cairo

She's lying half-clad on a hotel bed
reading *The Lover* when her Razrphone
buzzes. A smoky baritone voice asks,
Are you wearing cotton panties?

I never wear cotton panties, she answers.
Where did you get this number? A hint
of magnolia seeps from her deliberate words.

Are you wearing panties at all?
He asks in a nonchalant tone.

Is this an obscene phone call?
She rolls onto her stomach, eyes
the storm clouds roiling the downtown
skyline outside her Adolphus window.

Do you want it to be? he asks.

I want you to be more imperious.
Don't ask so many questions.

After a long silence he continues.
Tell me something about yourself.
Tell me something sad.

I've been in Cairo, she whispers.
I haven't felt rain on my skin
in six months. She disconnects him,
tosses the phone onto her bed.

She gazes outside at the ominous storm
and, shifting her balance to one hip,
waits for the phone to buzz again.

Hotel San Jose, Austin

The room is minimalist décor, the walls
parchment thin. Southside noises leak in—
backfire of an old Ford on Congress Ave,
headboard rhythmically banging the wall,
squeaky bedsprings next door. A woman
caught in the throes of *la petit mort*
howls like a wild dog.

Unable to suppress laughter, we cling
hysterically to each other, naked beneath
the sheets. I can't regain composure,
get back to our own love-making. You grab
my head, pull me down, and my tongue
finds your smooth minimalist center.

Everything's OK on the LBJ

I drive the 281 west
to Texas Hill Country,
find the ranch
on the hidden banks

of the Pedernales,
summer's sunscald
offering a rare glimpse
of the old man caught
with his hair grown long
and unkempt.

He sprawls in a field
of purple wildflowers,
at play with his grandkids.
He wears a peaceful smile
on his weathered face

as if content, the iron
yoke of the World's
Most Powerful Man
lifted from him forever,

the White House years
now fading in the indian
paintbrush and bluebonnets.

Twenty-Eights

Twenty-eight months passed
before she returned to Austin,
walked down The Drag, stopped
at the University Newsstand.
She pretended to browse magazines
but her hands shook. She couldn't
turn the pages. She felt the ominous
clock tower looming behind her,
28 stories tall, its shadow falling
across her back like cross-hairs
in the scope of Whitman's rifle.
The crack of shots rang out
in her memory, the slow-motion
fall of a man, her own frantic drop
behind a curbed Nash Rambler.
She flinched at 28 rifle pops, watched
a blood-pool seep from beneath
the man's head onto a Batman
comic book. She remembered how life
faded from his eyes, how they glazed
over, unaware. It seemed forever
before help came, dragged them out,
but she remembered looking at her
watch. Only 28 minutes had passed.

A Graffiti of Bats

rise from beneath Congress Ave Bridge
as if fired from cannons—
tens of thousands Mexican free-tails
mostly female, pregnant migrants.

They bank left in plump formation
spin east above Lady Bird Lake
seeking dinner— countless insects
unaware their pending fate.

Swarms of flapping wings
shape-shift into twister clouds, swirling
ribbons of vaporous vampires
escaping a monstrous movie screen.

All summer pups are born
in dark crevices beneath the bridge,
fill evening skies, learn to prey
until autumn summons them south

back across the Rio Grande
like snowbirds wintering till April,
then return to Austin's bridge, birth
new brood in the Land of Plenty.

Bésame in Austin

I won't lie to you. Since the Pan American
conventions in the '60s, traipsing the capitol
grounds with some good-looking gal is one
of my favorite Austin traditions. It ranks above
checking into the downtown Driskell, breakfast
and Bloody Marys at Cisco's, catching a sunset
bat swarm beneath Congress Avenue bridge—
all rituals no sane man would abandon.

The capitol rotunda is a *whispering gallery*
where I climb the stairs to an upper floor,
stand on one side of its circumference, whisper
to a girl on the other side *Bésame*.
She hears me clearly and grins. We stroll
to the Heroes of the Alamo monument where
I point out two fallen martyrs with my namesake.
Under the bronze Texan wielding his rifle,
I steal a kiss. What the hell's tradition worth
if it doesn't include kissing? Bet you already
figured that out. Bet you think on some of those
evenings, I don't go home alone.

Buda Woman

No more swaggering struts down Paris runways,
no more insolent airs at photo shoots. Not
for twenty years. Now she drinks Shiner
from longneck bottles, wears cowboy boots,
is still as pretty as when magazine covers
featured her face. She never bothers with makeup.

On the road to her ranch, three miles
off Buda Highway, she painted signs:
19 MPH and WE LIVE A SLOW LIFE HERE.
She loves to sit in a porch swing, listen to hoot
owls, clicking cicadas, distant train whistles—
a melodious symphony orchestrated
beneath a bone white moon.

My favorite photo of her is one in an open
leather jacket – no blouse, no bra,
only a smile as big as Texas. She claims
she hates it, but signed it for me anyway,
the dark ink looming over her image.

Old Chapel in the Woods

Evening sun grows bored burning the sky,
casts cool shadows on Festival Hill.
It's said the spirit of Edythe Bates Old
delights at sitting inside the ancient Methodist
sanctuary listening to chamber music
and poetry recitals. An arts patron, she paid
to move this chapel and its ancient pipe organ
sixteen miles from La Grange to Round Top.

Never tiring of the performances,
as darkness rustles surrounding trees,
she sits near the hand-carved pulpit,
closes her eyes, nods like she did at Julliard.
A fragrant incense assuages the senses
of artists lifting their voices inside
the burnished-wood chapel. Pleased,
she hums like a cat purring with pleasure
when stroked behind its ears.

Best Bitch

leaps from the truck
nose lowered and sniffing,
finds the perfect patch of grass,
squats, takes care of business.

In the Astrodome, she breaks
into graceful trot, head held high
with the attitude of a goddess.
The others, mere canines,
shuffle, their handlers pimping
them up while she executes
a nonchalant flop onto the ground
and feigns boredom.

She rises on cue, strides the ring,
mesmerizes the judges who can't
tear their eyes from her.
All competition fades in the trail
of her elegant strut. She stops
at runway's end, calmly waits
approval and the Best of Breed
blue ribbon. She knows.

Back in the truck, she lies down,
rides to the hill country kennel,
dreams of a plunge in the tank.
Then crawling out, she shakes
her fur and rolls in the mud,
again just one of the hounds.

Red Tractor

I drove through back roads Texas,
endless miles of flatland farms.
An old man atop a bright red tractor
plowed rows in a black dirt field.
He wore blue overalls and a wide-
brimmed hat shielding eyes and face
from a callous white sun.

Beneath a nearby elm
his cherry red Cadillac sat,
a young woman spread
on a blanket across the hood.
She wore cutoff jeans
and a yellow tank top
as she watched him plow.

I imagined his good luck
if when he finished
he might whisk her to town,
watch her change into a tiny
green bikini. Maybe bask
poolside, sip a salty margarita,
grin when he sees her lips
reaching for his mouth.

Texas Vampires

A flurry of wings swarm
through moss covered holes
in the roof of old Paramount Theatre.
Curling upside down, creatures hang
from ceiling fixtures in the projection booth.
Hidden from sun's blistering tongue,
sleep slaps them senseless.

Come Saturday morning, ancient ones
drop onto dusty Century projectors.
Insomniac bats morph into film buffs,
watch matinee movies until dusk.
They love Bela Lugosi in *Devil Bat*,
and David Bowie in *The Hunger*
with Deneuve and Sarandon making love.
But it's Polanski's *Fearless Vampire Killers*
that drives them wild, sends them
into wing-flapping frenzies when Sharon Tate
takes off her clothes and vamps for them.

So far, six teenage girls, a meter maid,
one horn-rimmed librarian have come up
missing. Speculation is they're secluded
in a Fort Worth home for unwed mothers.
No one knows who the father is, but town
folks are keeping suspicious eyes on
a buck-toothed Burleson projectionist.

Crossing the Border

A map of Mexico covers
my office wall, bright red dots
marking destinations I've tasted
like cherry sprinkles decorating
a *Tres Leches* cake.

Cactus in a terra cotta pot
soaks up sun rays falling through
my window. Ants crawl methodically
from pot to map, crossing the border
just above Tijuana.

I sink my feet into the carpet
beneath my desk, six inches deep
in Rosarito Beach sand. Eyes closed,
I'm transported to a canvas chair
shaded by a Dos Equis umbrella.

But the sound of 18-wheelers
screaming on the five o'clock freeway
jars me back to reality. I google
Three-Day Getaways Near Dallas,
sigh, and frugally plan my weekend.

Speeding Past the Zoo

His long tongue flicking
like a middle finger at birds
and planes, a gargantuan giraffe
dominates the Oak Cliff landscape
as cars race across the Trinity.
Motorists flee as if escaping a T. Rex
marauding through Jurassic Park.
When caught speeding they swear
in court their fear of doom while driving
beneath the shadow of the howling
monster caused them to break the law.
They insist eerie screeches scared them
into ignoring the speed limit.

This defense has not held up one single
time in traffic court for offenders
explaining to the judge their reason
for speeding, but it might explain why
I-35 alongside the Dallas Zoo
makes a perfect speed trap.

Cold March Day at Stevie Ray's Grave

The air turned grey, the grass brown,
a cruel wind nipped at the corners.
Laurel Land a blustery urban prairie
the day we paid our respects.

Kevin, flown in from California, kneeling,
a monolith as blue as his jeans and sweater,
so still not a poem stirred inside him.

Stevie Ray's grave, hard granite spread
thick over silence. His guitar did not weep,
their strings did not wail. Nothing
uttered a sound save a sudden whiff
whispering *He's gone*.

Kathy Jack's Backyard

Two AM, a screaming guitar
guts the night. Music explodes
from an abandoned garage
converted to West Dallas'
most notorious lesbian bar—
Kathy Jack's Backyard Grill.

On stage, clad in black-leather
with skull rings gilding her fingers,
struts Bianca from Rio, baddest
blues guitarist in Texas. Black magic
flows from her hands as she strokes
the strings. No one plays a Strat
like she does, no one draws
such frenzied crowds.

Both gays and straights, women
and men, all ages, bump shoulders,
grind hips as Bianca casts
her bluesy spell, mesmerizing
a mob like Stevie Ray once did.
She brings out the In Crowd,
who push and shove to stand
near her. Get there early, dare
thrust your way into the storm.

Appreciating Art On a Sunday Afternoon

Like chiseled ice her cold brown eyes
followed me from painting to painting—
Orosco, Kahlo, Rivera, the *Modern Masters
of Mexico* at Dallas' Art Museum.
Chilled breath hung in the air.

I shivered and rubbed my hands together
ravenous for warmth or invitation.
Provocation hid beneath her surface,
desire barely revealed but visible.

I closed the exhibit room door,
strolled boldly into her space.
Her face wore an unrelenting stare
that told me she knew why I was coming.
Her expression declared, *How dare you
think I'll let you.*

But something in the shift of her hip,
in the way her hand touched her skirt
told me she wouldn't resist. I watched
her defenses open, flecks of heat
in her eyes rose to the frozen surface,
threatened to fracture the ice.

I backed her into a wall, placed my hands
on each side of her expressionless face.
You're playing with fire, I whispered
staring at a mole on her chin.

Then burn me, she taunted
and opened her lips for my kiss.

You Can Leave Your Hat On

At night she wears tassels and G-string
beneath a nun's black habit, dances round
a pole at Million Dollar Saloon. Beer-guzzling
men howl and egg her on with folded bills.

Late mornings she suns by a Cedar Springs
pool clad in string bikini and floppy-brimmed hat,
reading Lorca and Neruda. Same as at night, men
drink her in, traverse her body with their eyes.

I rub oil into her skin, ask why she always wears
a nun's habit. She sheds her bra, stares at me
from beneath her hat as if I'm loony, genuflects
and grins. *I'm Catholic. It's the least I can do.*

Departures

Life has a habit of running laps
on a never-ending track.

A DFW terminal lounge, I watch you
bid goodbye to your mother—
a woman closer to my age than yours.
Time has thickened her figure and inked
wrinkles under her eyes. You, stylish
and fit, so trim you're a sharp knife blade
in your white pants, peck a dismissive
kiss on her cheek, eager to resume
your fast-lane adventures. The generation
gap has set in, I see it on both your faces.

She boards her plane and you return
to me, slip your hand into mine,
give my fingers an intimate squeeze.
I wonder how long I have before you feel
the same about me – dismissive, detached,
eager to banish me into my archaic cave.

Father Farewell

Who is this old man
with wild grey hair
lying lifeless in bed
whose empty eyes
stare into death
that will not come?
His blanched lips
move in silent
conversation
with no one
I can see nor hear
while tendrils
of medication drip
life-support
into veins collapsed
from far too many
needles.

I say *Pull the plug!*
Let him go
to his well-deserved
peace.

This is that same
virile stallion
who once mounted
women like brood
mares, tossed down
tequila shots
while shaking his fist
in the face of God.
The man who's
bequeathed
to me a hundred
faithless whores.

Attention Deficit

An eager sea gull pecking
a discarded package of Cheeto crumbs,
and craving the crunch that would add
that lighten-up moment to his day

looks up in time to see a crumpled
piece of paper cartwheeling
down the beach that may have been
a tumbleweed escaped from Marfa

where a Vietnamese waitress serves
rib-eye to a rancher who smothers it
in Tabasco watching her walk away
like a slinky wave returning to the sea.

Mogen David and Fifty Shades

A snotty little cloud, high and mighty
wearing Dress Greys all afternoon,
parks over South Padre's beach crowd.

Two women stand between its shadow
and a foamy surf, tattle-tonguing about
the preacher's wife. They whisper how

they spied her in Island Market sneaking
two bottles of Mogen David into her cart.
Who's she trying to fool? they gaff. *It's not*

even Passover! They cluck their tongues,
gnarly toes buried in cool coarse sand. Down
beach the preacher's wife relaxes beneath

a palm, sips her wine, devours *Fifty Shades
of Grey*, concentrating on the erotic words,
not her exposed skin turning shades of red.

She's unconcerned how fickle clouds
and church wags behave on summer days.
She fantasizes instead of wild love-making.

Sniggering Dolphins

Uncle Ed's big bulbous nose
glowed like boiled crawfish
as he leaned over a ferry rail
crossing Redfish Bay. He peered
into Gulf green waters, then yelled
There's one! There's one!
his stubby finger jutting out.

One grey dorsal fin broke the surface.
Then another! A pod of bottle-nosed
dolphins, all slippery and shiny, leaped
above the swells. We heard loud *PUFF!s*
as they forced air through their blow holes,
riding waves rolling from beneath
the bow, racing us to Mustang Island.

Seems a lifetime ago, but I still think
of Uncle Ed when I ride the ferry
to Port Aransas. I see him exuberant,
pointing his finger, and I swear I hear
those dolphins snigger as they speed
ahead of us across the bay.

Winged Sonata

Swooping
in graceful flight
a blue heron

snatched a poem
from the Gulf
and soared

into the concerto
of a setting sun
sprinkling poetry

like musical notes
onto my blue silk
imagination.

Breakfast on the Beach

A drenched seagull hip hops
beneath tables, snatches soggy
scraps from the puddled floor.
I watch over coffee cup steam
as he bounds to a door
and weighs whether
dashing into the storm
is a survivable notion.

Outside the pavilion, rain throws
sideway tantrums and fire hose
spray. The tempest din drowns
Willie's *Bloody Mary Morning*
pouring from ceiling speakers.
I can't see the sun climb out
of the Gulf, can't hear the frenzied
waves roll in, but I'm determined
to enjoy early morning beach
breakfast and watch the seagull
critique the soppy presentation.

Finn's Grill & Icehouse

Chris Craft's stereo spews Clapton riffs
and I jack it up to hear how a Fender
sounds in a master's hands. Wooden
dock posts sport pelicans who nod
their heads, nap, or perhaps pray for me
as I sing *If you wanna get down,*
down on the ground, Cocaine...

After a day spent reeling in redfish and snook
I consider dropping by Finn's Grill & Icehouse
where beer is served so cold ice forms
on the sides of tall thick mugs and seafood
is brought to the table by long-legged sirens
covered in colorful tattoos and pithy
fishing-town attitudes.

I watch another Technicolor sunset
paint the Gulf of Mexico bright pink and purple
and catch glimpses of bay dolphins leaping.
A craggy old pelican stares at me as if to ask
Why the hell don't you turn loose of city life
and grab this spot on the Texas coast?
I wonder why myself.

Cormorants

Matagorda Bay and cormorants
regally perch, flocks of them, black
as feathered cats, awaiting

sunrise breezes bringing fish scent.
Their hunger aroused, they morph
into winged panthers, leap skyward,

plunge beneath waters to feed, frenzied
like pigs, grunting. Engorged they
return to jutting rocks, spread heavy

wet wings to dry. Bellies full, they bask
in morning sunshine, drift into slumber,
big docile birds again.

Lazy Autumn Afternoon

I sip Long Island Tea from a jelly jar,
watch an old hound circle three times
then flop in the shade of a dumpster.
A murder of crows perched atop
a parked Mercedes studies him
and the crate of Minute Maid lemons
rotting in the sun behind him. The dog's
eyes close and two Heckle and Jeckles
scratch their chins, weigh the risk.
They flap their wings and scramble
brashly to the lemons, peck fermented
pulp until the sky psychedelically changes
colors. A woman in tight black pants
and a sleeveless Nelson Cruz jersey strolls
to the Mercedes, slides onto the front seat.
The old hound opens one eye, yawns
as she slowly drives away. The crows
feverishly gulp their potent lemon juice
and I mosey back inside, refill my jelly
jar, turn on my TV in time to watch
the Cowboys kick off another
gut-wrenching 8-and-8 season.

One Year After Her Father Died

I picked her up at the airport
the day she flew in from L.A.
and drove her to the cemetery
where she burned Sho-ko incense.
Later we stopped at Dickey's,
bought her father's favorite ribs,
took them back to my place—
a studio apartment so cramped
we sat on the balcony to eat
and reminisce about his life.
Afterward, we slipped inside,
watched seasons of *Nikita*.
She took off all but her panties,
unpinned her hair and let it fall.
I poured Chilean Cabernet.
She wouldn't make love to me,
claimed she'd come out of the closet,
but she sprawled on my bed
showing off her perfect breasts
and commented on how sexy
Maggie Q looked. At the end
of each episode, she leaned in
and bit me on the upper arm.
My biceps were purple bruises
by the end of season two.

Sleeping On the Silver Eagle

All night jagged lightning flashes,
angry rain pounds the train windows.
Across the aisle a mestizo woman moans
in fitful dreams – perhaps coyotes
running through prickly cactus.

In my earbuds Elton John sings
Hold me closer tiny dancer,
count the headlights on the highway.
I count cars zooming the interstate
until my eyes close. The train's
doleful whistle cries me to sleep.

Two hundred rickety miles later
I awaken, folded tight into a creased
origami. Light rain beads the window,
dawn illuminates San Antonio station.
The woman's seat now empty, I see
a ragdoll cat outside hunkered beneath
the station doorway. I stand and stretch,
stumble toward the diner car jonesing
for a mug of hot coffee.

At Six Flags Cinema

A girl in short plaid skirt
sits on the back row, bucket
of yellow-buttered popcorn
warm between her knees.
Leonardo DiCaprio, in brooding
persona of Romeo, dominates
the midnight screen. His baby-faced
good looks race her engines
as he struts a fictional Verona Beach
wielding his Dagger-brand pistol
instead of a sword. She knows
her young heartthrob will land
in trouble before movie's end.
But its bad boys like him who ignite
passion into tinsel town romance
and make her believe Willie the Bard
was the best damn screenwriter
who ever lifted a pen!

Along Randol Mill Road

On September Sundays
navigating a pickup truck
from the Great Temple
Nolan Ryan built
to Jerry Jones' billion-dollar
Mother Ship down the street
can require up to an hour,
a ritual rich with aromas—
burning charcoal, crackling
grease, hot links, sizzling beef—
incense of tailgate sacraments
on a strip of holy real estate
where Big Boy Games
are not mere sports,
but a fanatically rabid religion,
war hymns and all.

Action in the Bleachers

I crack peanut shells, drop debris
on my Nikes and try hard to fake
interest in the game, but the Rangers'
batters aren't helping. They've missed
every pitch thrown their way. Oakland's
ace seems headed for a clean sweep.
Looks like the highlight of tonight's
outing is an Asian chick holding court
in the seat next to me.

Drop-dead gorgeous, all cleavage
and legs, wearing giant purple shades,
she's on her fourth beer and spouting
useless information to anyone who'll listen,
things like *Did you know those raised
highway pavement markers are called
Bott's Dots because they're named after
the engineer who invented them?*

Bored with her endless prattle as well
as the game, I stand and shake shells
from my shoes. She looks up at me
as if I should speak, so I say to her
*Did you know Nolan Ryan never won
the Cy Young Award in his 27 years
pitching in the major leagues?*
And with a deadpan face, she asks
Who's Nolan Ryan?

Los Jarros

I eat breakfast Sunday mornings
at a hole-in-the-wall on Randol Mill Road,
my table next to the window. Outside,

raised on a rusted tubular pole, a sign:
LOS JARROS, and its cluster of jugs,
the restaurant's namesake.

I'll admit, I have no imagination,
no desire to change my routine. Always
the same feast for me – chips and salsa,

Chilaquiles, corn tortillas, coffee, and chests.
Yes, the food is *grande,* but the well-endowed
waitresses even better. All of them young,

friendly, dressed in black slacks and green
blouses tight as snakeskins. With each one
I hold a gaze, lure a smile, try not to stare.

Los Jarros the sign proclaims, assorted jugs
decorate walls and tables. But they're not
the ones drawing all the attention.

Evening Alchemy

The gangly girl behind Asian Market's
fish counter chops sea trout and squid,
scrapes scales from yellowfin tuna.
Austere as egg noodles in her homely
white frock and plain canvas cap,
she scurries sink to counter to table.
Her expressionless almond eyes stare
from behind thick lenses.

Five o'clock she punches out, scrubs
hands with lemon soap, trades her frock
for a little black dress. She lets down
long shiny hair and spritzes Calvin Klein.
Contacts replace glasses and she smiles
approval into the mirror. A choreographed
hip-swiveling walk transports her
to a popular Arlington bar.

She captures glances as she lolls blasé
on a lounge, long-legged and laughing,
basks in the spotlight of attention. Pleased
with herself, she is a *new* woman— confident,
charming, a pearl released from its shell.

Hospital Vamp

Five AM, the door flies open
and she bursts into my room,
her lab coat flapping like a cape.
She mutters gleefully, *I've come
to take your blood*, tightens
a tourniquet around my arm,
glides her pointy finger over
engorged veins. Finding what
she wants, she whispers *Oh! This
one will do!* Her Bela Lugosi cackle
coaxes a needle into my flesh,
blood shoots up the tube. I lie
in helpless surrender while she
gazes into my eyes. She smiles,
snaps the rubber tourniquet
off my arm, flies from the room—
a bat rushing back to her cave
before sunlight arrives. I'm left
beneath the morphine drip,
listening to her laughter fade.

Del Rio, Two AM

The Texas Eagle pulls in
and I half-expect I'll hear
Wolfman Jack's gravely howl
blast from a half-million-watt
illegal tower in Acuña across
the Rio Grande. Back in the day,
a car traveling LA to New York
never lost this station's broadcasts
so powerful that birds flying
too close dropped from the sky.

Weary passengers stepping
off for a smoke are warned
Don't touch the fence—
a ten-foot chain-link
sporting a sign: *Val Verde
Correctional Facility.*
An Uzi-toting soldier tosses
a butt against the wire,
watches it spark and char black.
No one has to be warned twice.

When the train leaves
the station an old cowboy
listening to a rock song
gazes out the window.
Behind him, town lights
fade. He flings his headset
and curses under his breath,
*I wouldn't play this music
at a Del Rio dogfight!*
A sirocco whips the tower,
its haunting sound resonant
as a wolf howl.

Busting Out of Balmorhea

Hell-bent
for Mexico
90 miles an hour
in a Hemi Head
halfway between
Monahans
and Marfa, shirt
blown open
while the Stones
lay down *Hip Shake*
on the stereo
like it's 1972.

Tumbleweeds
bebop
to Mick Taylor's
guitar licks
and a Warner Bros
Giant sky
stretches
like a silk serape
from the Guadalupe
mountains to
the Chisos.

Gotta make
Lajitas
before the music
changes
from rock'n'roll
to Mariachi
and the last
boat crosses
the smug
Rio Grande.

Crossing the Desert

The Angus steak burger would taste better
without the chipotle sauce, but this train
runs Texas to Mexico so I'll take it like a man.
I'd prefer the taste of guacamole spread,
the cool slick kind Bianca whips up.
To be more specific, a batch like she made
for my fortieth birthday and smeared
all over my chest. Well, you can guess
what happened next, and I think about it
as I stare out the dining car window.
I see buzzards perched on saguaros
which reminds me of old Road Runner
cartoons, the way the vultures sit
with shoulders hunched when Wile E
Coyote blasts by on his way to get hit
by a train crossing the desert. This has
nothing to do with guacamole or chipotle
sauce, it's just the waitress serving lunch
reminds me of a skinny road runner with
her blue-grey pants and orange knee-high
socks and the way she struts like nothing
can ever touch her. And nothing can.
After all, I'm no threat, and Poncho Villa
was killed a hundred years ago begging
his men to make up something to tell
people he said when he died,
something that sounds cooler than
Vámanos! Let's run that stop sign.

A Night in Marfa with Rock Hudson

In far west Texas I check into Hotel Paisano—
the Rock Hudson suite overlooking a pool.
I kick off my boots, slide off my jeans,
splash across bathroom tiles. I shower,
collapse on a bed, weary after driving
500 miles from Dallas.

Lying in this hotel, in this town, reminds me
of times mom worked the Loop-12 Drive-in
and *Giant* played all summer. Each night
my brother and I sprawled on a mattress
in the back of her car watching James Dean
and Liz Taylor steal every scene. We could
quote practically the entire movie.

Most of all I remember cringing each time
we watched Rock Hudson get his ass kicked
in that roadside café defending a Mexican family's
right to dine there. No one's life turned out
the way the hero wanted but his celluloid words
burned like high beams in the desert.

Cats & Colors

I step outside Hotel Holland
after an alfalfa rain, wearing new eyes
beneath an oil-painted Renoir sky.
The portrait features brush strokes of blues,
crisp film-noir grays and whites. Cloud
shadows slide down sepia mountains,
roll onto sun-colored town streets.
West Texas never looked so clean!

My stroll across this artist's pallet
of vivid morning hues, past shops,
cafés, galleries and bars, reveals Alpine's
silent hidden citizens— cats, dozens of them,
napping in shaded nooks and cool dark
corners, waiting for the sun to stretch
its warm fingertips, scratch furry bellies,
rouse them so folks can sound the call
to late morning breakfasts.

Blues Song

A sidewalk shoeshine stand
smudged and weatherworn
sits deserted out front
an Alpine café.
A bass guitar leans
against a wooden bench
left to hum in the wind.

Inside the café, a young musician
ignores lunch and grins
as an old shoeshine man blows
a tune on his mouth harp.
A blues song is being born
over cornbread and beans.

Dinosaur

I drive my 12-year old car
through campus, turn left
on Nedderman, stop at Cooper.
Across the street I see Texas Hall
and remember Bob Dylan's concert
back when I was a student— the one
where, dressed in a black cowboy outfit,
he rocked all his ballads and crooned
his rock songs like slow tunes.
I glance at the class ring on my finger.
The word *REBELS* catches my eye,
not *MAVERICKS*— today's politically correct
mascot. I watch the beautiful students
tumble out of University Hall, ants
spreading in all directions clad in shorts,
tank tops, sandals. They're all so young!
One of them, a 20-year-old coed
saunters up to my car. She opens the door,
slides onto the front seat beside me.
Smiling, she greets me: *Hi, Grandpa.*
Thanks for giving me a ride this afternoon.
No problem, I assure her, and pull
into the stream of traffic.
How're you feeling today? she asks.
A wry grin creeps across my wrinkled face.
Feeling obsolete, I mumble,
like an old dinosaur.

Strawberries on a Warm December Evening

I brought you fresh strawberries, I said.
She smiled and opened her mouth.

Do you like strawberries? I asked.
Sometimes, she answered, and the glaze
cleared from her eyes.

With the blade of my pocketknife,
I hurriedly cut away the leafy ends
of each plump succulent delight,
fed her fruit from my fingers.
She chewed with a toothless grin.
Her eyes watched me intensely
as though seeing me for the first time.
You're my son, aren't you?

I continued to feed her the tender
red fruit, wipe juice from her chin,
answer questions about her grandchildren
and where in Texas they lived.

After eating, she closed her eyes,
said *Thank you. Now I think I'll sleep.*
And just as she slipped into peace
she smiled again, said
That was sweet.

About the Author

Travis Blair lives down the road from the University of Texas campus in Arlington where he earned a BA in English Lit. After a lengthy career in the movie business, he took up writing poetry. Author of two books, *Train to Chihuahua* and *Little Sandwiches*, his poems have appeared in literary journals throughout the United States, England, South Africa, and Australia. He formerly served as President of the Dallas Poets Community and is a member of the Writers League of Texas. He has two daughters, five grandkids, and hides from them frequently in Manhattan and Mazatlán.